Meet the dinosaurs

Before you start reading *Spiky Stegosaurus*, let's meet its main characters. Who are they? What do they look like? And where did they live?

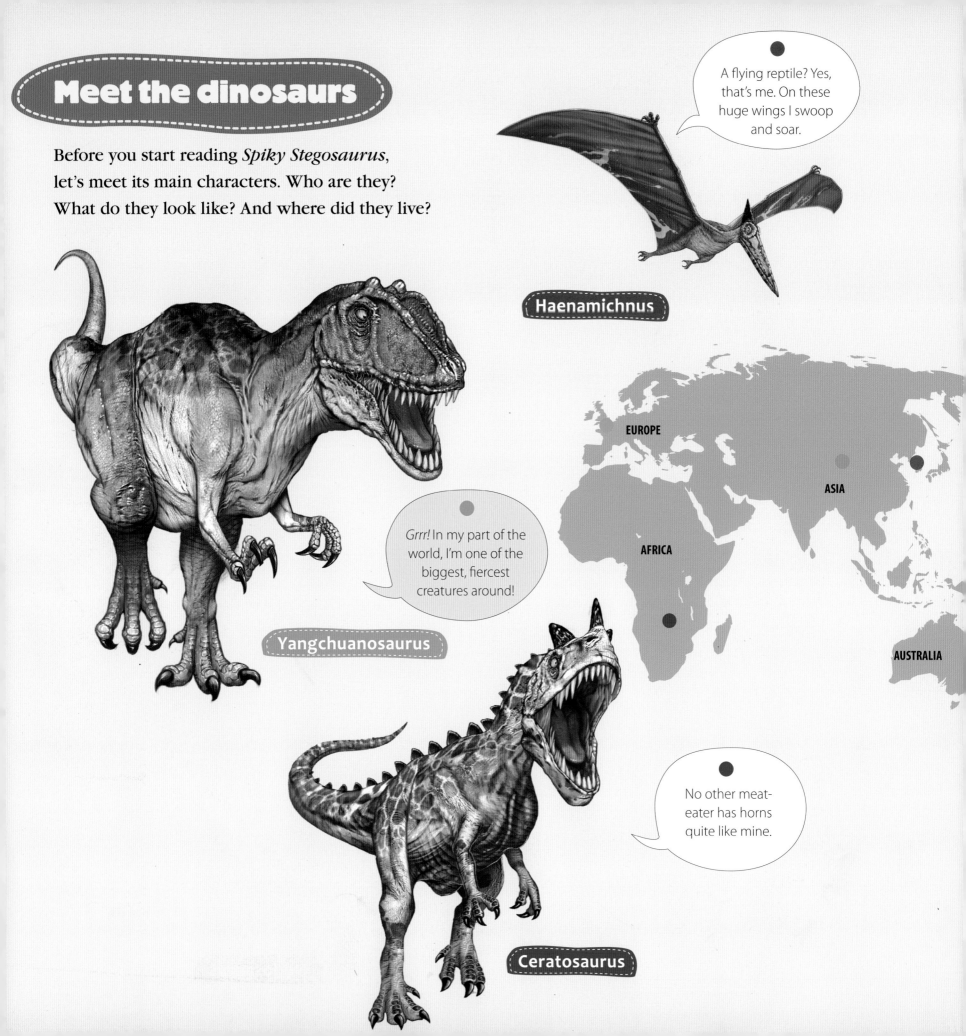

A flying reptile? Yes, that's me. On these huge wings I swoop and soar.

Haenamichnus

Grrr! In my part of the world, I'm one of the biggest, fiercest creatures around!

Yangchuanosaurus

EUROPE

ASIA

AFRICA

AUSTRALIA

No other meat-eater has horns quite like mine.

Ceratosaurus

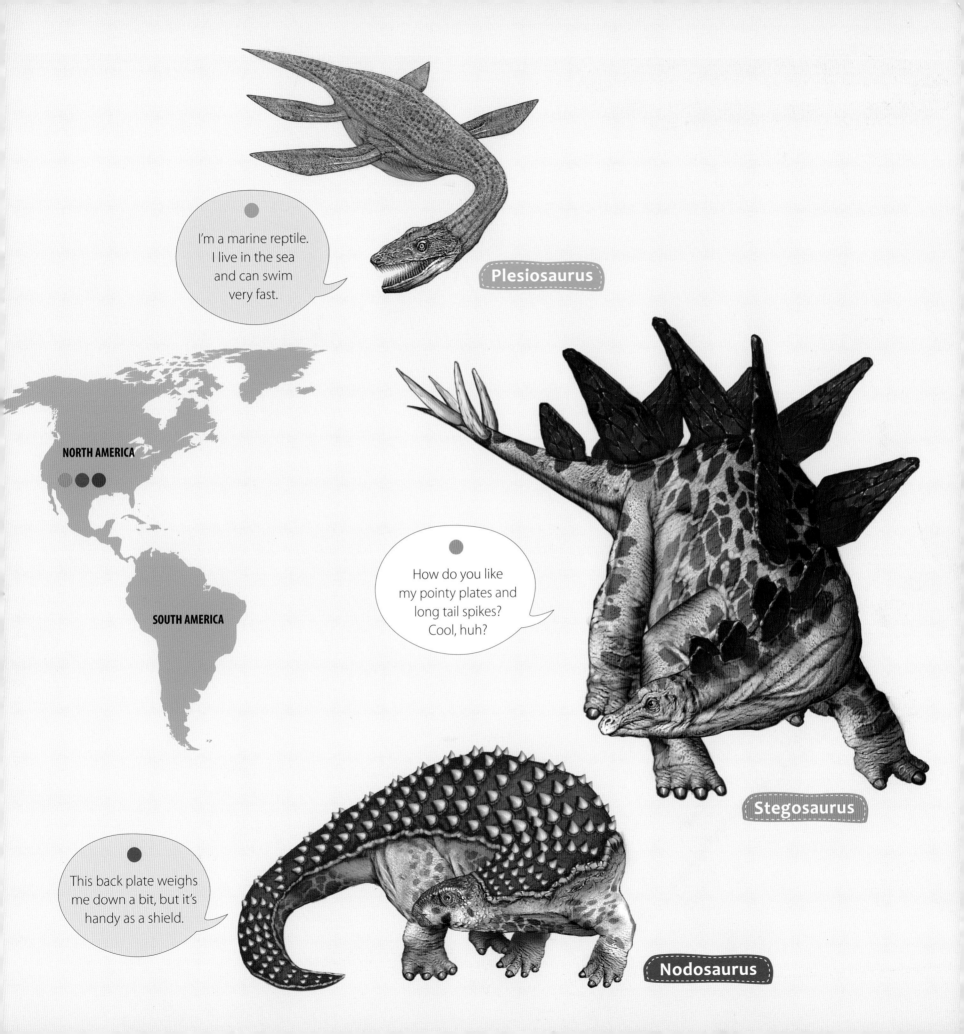

big & SMALL

Original Korean text and illustrations by Dreaming Tortoise
Korean edition © Aram Publishing

This English edition published by big & SMALL in 2016
by arrangement with Aram Publishing
English text edited by Scott Forbes
English edition © big & SMALL 2016

Distributed in the United States and Canada by
Lerner Publishing Group, Inc.
241 First Avenue North
Minneapolis, MN 55401 U.S.A.
www.lernerbooks.com

Photo credits:
Page 28, top: © Jose Maria Silveira Neto

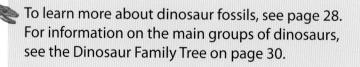

To learn more about dinosaur fossils, see page 28.
For information on the main groups of dinosaurs,
see the Dinosaur Family Tree on page 30.

Spiky
Stegosaurus

Stegosaurus

big & SMALL

Ceratosaurus

Two Ceratosaurus were about to attack an enormous Seismosaurus. Suddenly an Allosaurus charged toward one of them. Clearly it had its eye on the same prey.

No big meat-eater was likely to give up its prey without a fight. So what would happen next?

SEISMOSAURUS

GROUP: Sauropods
DIET: Plants
WHEN IT LIVED: Late Jurassic
WHERE IT LIVED: North America (USA)
LENGTH: 130 feet (40 meters)
HEIGHT: 20 feet (6 meters)
WEIGHT: 55 tons
(50 tonnes)

Ceratosaurus had powerful legs and sharp claws on its hands for getting a good grip on its prey. Its massive jaws could bite hard and hold fast, and its teeth were like sharp blades. On its head were two short horns — Ceratosaurus means "lizard with horns."

ALLOSAURUS

GROUP: Theropods
DIET: Meat
WHEN IT LIVED: Late Jurassic
WHERE IT LIVED: North America (USA) Europe
(Portugal), Africa (Tanzania), Australia
LENGTH: 25–40 feet (7.5–12 meters)
HEIGHT: 10–13 feet (3–4 meters)
WEIGHT: 1.1–2 tons
(1–1.8 tonnes)

One Ceratosaurus and the Allosaurus flew at each other, biting and ripping. After a violent struggle, the Ceratosaurus fell to the ground wounded.

But at that moment, the other Ceratosaurus dashed over and prepared to attack the Allosaurus. The Allosaurus had used up all its strength and knew it could not defeat two enemies at once. So it backed away, turned, and ran into the forest.

Ceratosaurus often hunted in packs. Working together, a group of Ceratosaurus could bring down a huge dinosaur such as Seismosaurus.

HEIGHT: 8 feet (2.5 meters)

LENGTH: 20–33 feet (6–10 meters)

WEIGHT: 1.1 tons (1 tonne)

WHEN IT LIVED: TRIASSIC | JURASSIC | CRETACEOUS

GROUP: Theropods

DIET: Meat

WHERE IT LIVED:
Africa (Tanzania),
North America (USA)

Nodosaurus

Two Nodosaurus took fright when they saw a Utahraptor approaching. But the Utahraptor didn't attack. It had remembered the last time it had tried to attack a Nodosaurus. It had broken a tooth on the plant-eater's bony back shield. It didn't want to do that again!

The name "Nodosaurus" means "knobbed lizard." The name refers to the many bumps on the dinosaur's back, like knobs.

10

Nodosaurus was one of the slowest dinosaurs. That was partly because the heavy plates on its back weighed it down. The plates were made of a tough, bony material and each one rose to a short, pointed knob or horn.

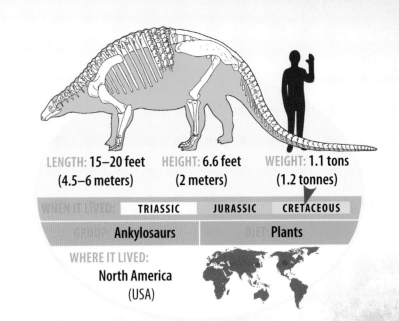

LENGTH: 15–20 feet (4.5–6 meters)	HEIGHT: 6.6 feet (2 meters)	WEIGHT: 1.1 tons (1.2 tonnes)

WHEN IT LIVED:	TRIASSIC	JURASSIC	CRETACEOUS

GROUP: Ankylosaurs	DIET: Plants

WHERE IT LIVED:
North America
(USA)

UTAHRAPTOR

GROUP: Theropods
DIET: Meat
WHEN IT LIVED: Early Cretaceous
WHERE IT LIVED: North America (USA)
LENGTH: 20–23 feet (6–7 meters)
HEIGHT: 6.6 feet (2 meters)
WEIGHT: 0.55–9.5 tons
(0.5–0.85 tonnes)

The Nodosaurus went back to munching on leaves.
But then a ferocious Acrocanthosaurus appeared.
The Nodosaurus thought they might not be
so lucky this time.

They crouched down to protect their soft underparts
and waited for the Acrocanthosaurus to attack.
But it just growled and walked away. Even a huge,
fearsome dinosaur would think twice about trying
to bite through Nodosaurus's spiky shield.

Haenamichnus

SAY IT:
Hay-na-MIK-nus

Haenamichnus pushed itself off the sea cliff, and flew out over the sea, soaring through the wide blue sky. Soon it spotted the back of a fish breaking the surface of the sea. It swooped down in an instant and snatched the fish out of the water.

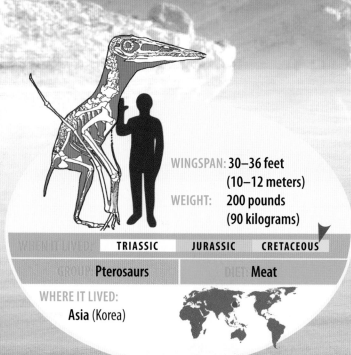

WINGSPAN:	30–36 feet (10–12 meters)
WEIGHT:	200 pounds (90 kilograms)

WHEN IT LIVED:	TRIASSIC	JURASSIC	CRETACEOUS

GROUP	Pterosaurs	DIET	Meat

WHERE IT LIVED:
Asia (Korea)

Pterosaurs were not dinosaurs, but flying reptiles. Haenamichnus was one of the largest pterosaurs in Asia. When it was on the ground, Haenamichnus walked on all four feet.

Stegosaurus

A Stegosaurus came out of the forest to enjoy the sunshine. An Allosaurus rushed toward it, flashing its fangs.

The Stegosaurus stood firm and swung its spiky tail at its attacker. The Allosaurus reeled back, moaning in pain. Then it turned away to nurse its wound.

16

HEIGHT: **23 feet**
(7 meters)

LENGTH: **30 feet**
(9 meters)

WEIGHT: **3.3–3.9 tons**
(3–3.5 tonnes)

WHEN IT LIVED: | TRIASSIC | JURASSIC | CRETACEOUS

GROUP: **Stegosaurs**   DIET: **Plants**

WHERE IT LIVED:
North America
(USA)

ALLOSAURUS

GROUP: Theropods
DIET: Meat
WHEN IT LIVED: Late Jurassic
WHERE IT LIVED: North America (USA),
Europe (Portugal), Africa (Tanzania), Australia
LENGTH: 25–40 feet (7.5–12 meters)
HEIGHT: 10–13 feet (3–4 meters)
WEIGHT: 1.6–3.3 tons
(1.5–3 tonnes)

Stegosaurus probably used the big, pointy plates on its back to attract a mate. But it may also have used them to control its body temperature. Blood vessels ran through the plates. So by turning the plates to face the sun, Stegosaurus could warm up. By turning them away from the sun, it could cool down.

When scientists first found Stegosaurus fossils, they thought the plates on its back must have lain flat, like the tiles on a roof. So they gave it the name Stegosaurus, which means "roofed lizard."

Plesiosaurus

SAY IT:
Plee-zee-oh-SAW-rus

The Plesiosaurus dived and tumbled in the sea, chasing and snapping up fish. Their long, slender bodies moved fast and easily under the water.

These marine reptiles lived in a very different world from the dinosaurs on dry land.

Plesiosaurus was the most common marine reptile during the early Jurassic Period. Its name means "near lizard."

As the Plesiosaurus swam along, they spotted some tuna. With a flap of their fins, they sped up and caught the tasty fish.

Plesiosaurus had sharp, slanted teeth, which helped it catch and hold onto fish and other slippery marine creatures, such as squid.

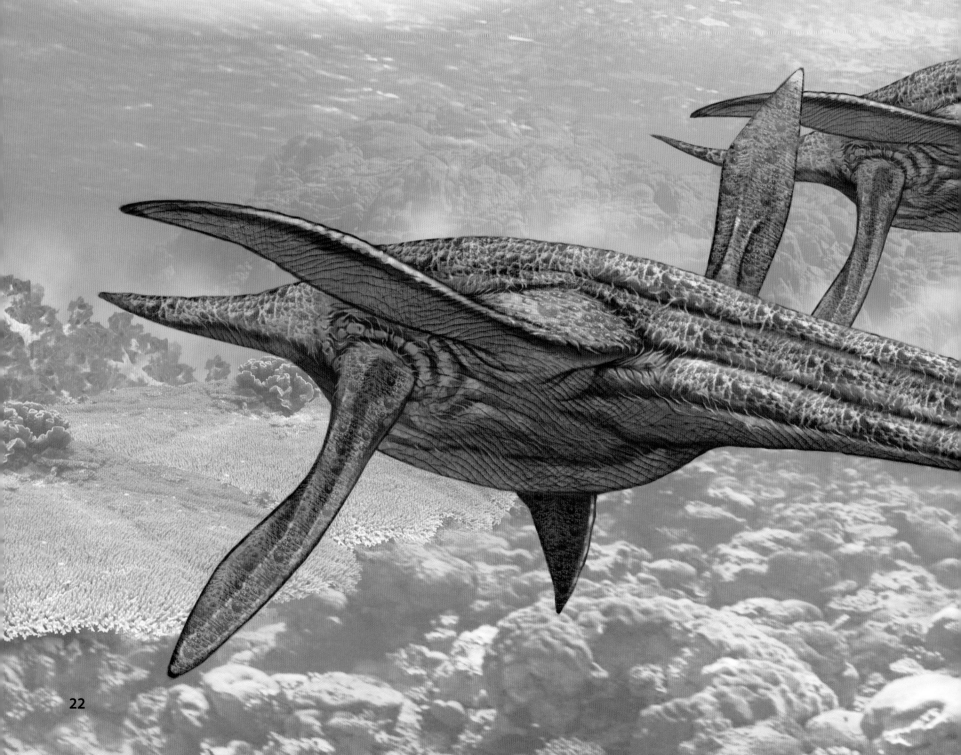

Plesiosaurus swallowed stones, which remained in its stomach. These may have helped it mash up and digest food. Or they may have made the bottom of its body heavier, so that it stayed upright in the water.

LENGTH: 10–16.5 feet (3–5 meters)

HEIGHT: 16 inches (40 centimeters)

WEIGHT: 0.5 tons (0.45 tonnes)

WHEN IT LIVED: TRIASSIC | JURASSIC | CRETACEOUS

GROUP: Plesiosaurs

DIET: Meat (sealife)

WHERE IT LIVED: Europe (UK, Germany)

Yangchuanosaurus

SAY IT:
Yang-choo-an-oh-SAW-rus

Yangchuanosaurus means "lizard from Yongchuan." This is the region in China where fossils of this dinosaur were first found.

A young female Yangchuanosaurus passed a pair of young males. The males pushed each other aside, trying to attract her attention. But the female Yangchuanosaurus took only a brief look at them and then walked on. It seemed she wasn't interested in either of them!

LENGTH: 33 feet (10 meters)

HEIGHT: 16.5 feet (5 meters)

WEIGHT: 1.1 tons (1 tonne)

WHEN IT LIVED:	TRIASSIC	JURASSIC	CRETACEOUS
GROUP: Theropods		DIET: Meat	

WHERE IT LIVED:
Asia (China)

The two male Yangchuanosaurus were getting hungry, so they set off on a hunt. They prowled through the forest, looking for prey, and soon they spotted a young Huayangosaurus. Attacking it from two sides, they quickly brought it to the ground. It was plenty for both of them to eat.

26

Yangchuanosaurus was one of the largest predators in what is now China during the mid- to late Jurassic Period. With its powerful jaws and strong teeth, it could easily kill other creatures, big and small. But it was a heavy dinosaur, so it could not run very fast.

HUAYANGOSAURUS

GROUP: Stegosaurs
DIET: Plants
WHEN IT LIVED: Mid-Jurassic
WHERE IT LIVED: Asia (China)
LENGTH: 15 feet (4.5 meters)
HEIGHT: 5 feet (1.5 meters)
WEIGHT: 1–1.1 tons
(0.9–1 tonne)

Dinosaur Fossils

Fossils are the remains of dinosaurs. They can be hard parts of dinosaurs, such as bones and teeth, that have slowly turned to stone. Or they may be impressions of bones, teeth, or skin preserved in rocks.

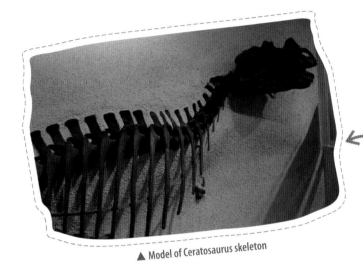

▲ Model of Ceratosaurus skeleton

Ceratosaurus

In 1883, two different dinosaur fossils were found together in a pit in the state of Colorado, USA. One of the fossils was of Allosaurus and the other was of Ceratosaurus. Scientists think they died during a fight, possibly over prey. These two types of dinosaurs lived in the same region at the same time, so they may have clashed regularly.

Nodosaurus

The first Nodosaurus fossils were found in the state of Wyoming, USA, in 1889. They were part of a skull and part of a backbone. This was enough for scientists to work out what the dinosaur looked like. A famous dinosaur hunter called Othniel Marsh gave the Nodosaurus its name. Later, more fossils were found in different parts of western North America, and these revealed a lot more about this dinosaur.

◄ Othniel Marsh

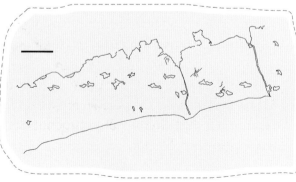

▲ Map of fossilized footprints of Haenamichnus

Haenamichnus

The full scientific name of this pterosaur is *Haenamichnus uhangriensis*. The name refers to two of the places in Korea where its fossilized footprints have been found: Haenam-gun and Uhang-ri. The dinosaur was first named and described in a scientific journal in 2002.

▲ Model of Stegosaurus skeleton

Stegosaurus

The first Stegosaurus fossil was found in Colorado, USA, in 1877. It was not a complete fossil, but scientist Othniel Marsh was still able to work out what kind of dinosaur it was and give it its name. Within the next few years, many other Stegosaurus fossils were found in the same district, including complete skeletons and skeletons of young Stegosaurus. These helped researchers learn much more about this dinosaur.

Plesiosaurus

Plesiosaurus fossils were first found in 1820 by a young English girl called Mary Anning. She lived on the coast in Dorset and was the daughter of a fossil collector, Richard Anning, one of the earliest dinosaur hunters — he was hunting for dinosaurs before the word "dinosaur" had been invented! Mary discovered her first important fossil, an ichthyosaur skull, when she was just 12 years old.

◀ A page from Mary Anning's journal recording her discoveries

Yangchuanosaurus

A builder stumbled across the first fossil of Yangchuanosaurus while he was working on the construction of a dam in Yongchuan, China, in 1977. The fossil was in excellent condition and it turned out that the rocks in the area were perfect for preserving fossils. Many more Yangchuanosaurus fossils were soon found.

▲ Model of Yangchuanosaurus skeleton

201 MILLION YEARS AGO

Yangchuanosaurus

THE DINOSAUR FAMILY TREE

Theropods (meat-eaters)

Saurischians (lizard-hipped dinosaurs)

Sauropods (long-necked plant-eaters)

Therizinosaurs (long-clawed dinosaurs)

Stegosaurs (plate-backed plant-eaters)

Huayangosaurus

Dinosaur ancestors

Ankylosaurs (armored plant-eaters)

Ornithischians (bird-hipped dinosaurs)

Ornithopods (two-legged plant-eaters)

Dinosaurs lived on Earth from about 245 million years ago until about 66 million years ago — long before the first humans. After the first dinosaurs appeared, they spread to all the continents and many different kinds of dinosaurs emerged. This chart shows the main groups of dinosaurs.

Pterosaurs (flying reptiles)

Ichthyosaurs (marine reptiles)

Plesiosaurus

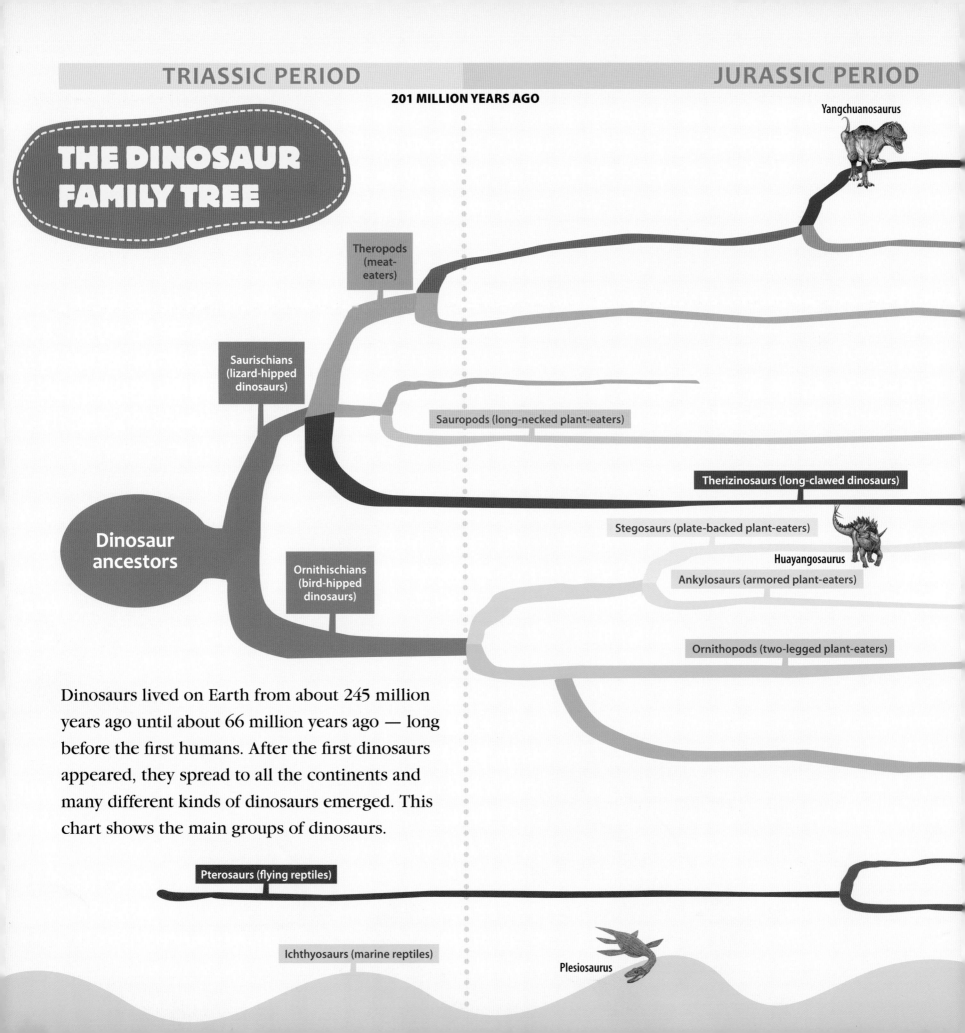

145 MILLION YEARS AGO

66 MILLION YEARS AGO

Carnosaurs (large meat-eaters)

Allosaurus

Acrocanthosaurus

Coelurosaurs (small meat-eaters)

Utahraptor

Ceratosaurus

Seismosaurus

Stegosaurus

Nodosaurus

Pachycephalosaurs (thick-skulled plant-eaters)

Ceratopsians (horned plant-eaters)

Haenamichnus